vmb
PUBLISHERS

TEXTS BY

ANGELA SERENA ILDOS

**project manager
and editorial director**
VALERIA MANFERTO DE FABIANIS

graphic design
CLARA ZANOTTI

graphic layout
MARIA CUCCHI

editorial coordination
ALBERTO BERTOLAZZI
GIADA FRANCIA
ENRICO LAVAGNO
CLAUDIA ZANERA

translation
RICHARD PIERCE

Published in the USA by
VMB Publishers®
An imprint of White Star, Italy
© 2004 WHITE STAR S.R.L.
VIA CANDIDO SASSONE, 22-24
13100 VERCELLI - ITALY
WWW.WHITESTAR.IT

● Africa. Lion cubs hiding in the grass watch the adults hunting.

ISBN 88-540-0116-3
REPRINTS:
1 2 3 4 5 6   08 07 06 05 04
Printed in China

CONTENTS

BABY ANIMALS

Cover East Africa. Lion cub with its mother. © C. and M. Denis Huot.

Back cover United States. A polar family. © N. Rosing/National Geographic Image Collection

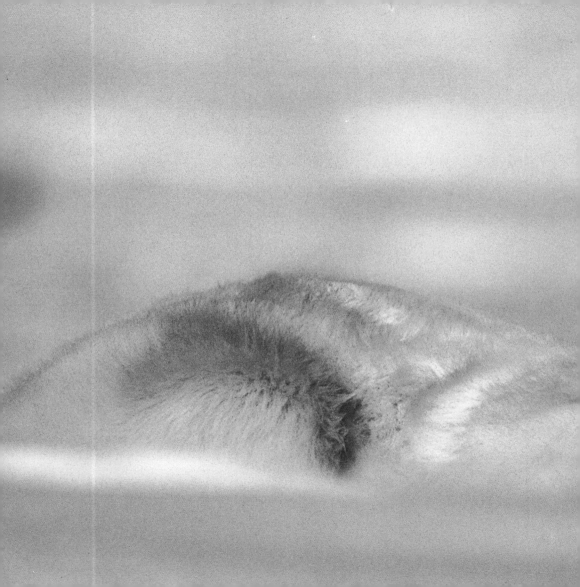

Introduction

EVERY YOUNG ANIMAL–BE IT A PUPPY, KITTEN, CUB, YEARLING OR CHICK–IS A PRECIOUS AND UNIQUE TREASURE, AND THERE IS NOTHING GREATER THAN THE LOVE THAT BONDS THE MOTHER AND HER YOUNG.

THIS BOND IS SO STRONG AND ALL-EMBRACING THAT ALL OTHER SENTIMENTS TAKE SECOND PLACE, EVEN THE INSTINCT OF SURVIVAL, EVEN THOSE BARRIERS THAT NATURE HAS CREATED AMONG THE VARIOUS SPECIES, WHICH HOWEVER FEROCIOUS THEY MAY BE, COLLAPSE WHEN AN ORPHAN SEEKS THE LOVE OF A NEW MOTHER. THE POWER OF THIS LOVE EXPLAINS WHY IN EVERY AGE AND EVERY CULTURE HUMANS HAVE SOUGHT THE COMPANY OF YOUNG ANIMALS

• United States. A gray wolf that is only a few days old.

Introduction

AND LOVE TAKING CARE OF THEM. YET THE BABY ANI-
MAL IS SO FRAGILE... IT IS BORN IN A RUTHLESS WORLD
MADE UP OF PREDATORS AND PREY, HUNGER, COLD,
DROUGHT, UNKNOWN DANGERS AND CALCULATED
RISKS, ARMED ONLY WITH A SWEET EXPRESSION AND
CURIOUS GLANCE. IS THIS ENOUGH? WILL IT SURVIVE?
AND WILL ITS CHARMING CLUMSINESS NOT GET IT INTO
TROUBLE? THE URGE TO HELP IT IS ONLY TOO NATURAL.
HOWEVER, WE MUST BEAR IN MIND THAT THIS HELP-
LESS CREATURE POSSESSES A GENETIC HERITAGE THAT
PROVIDES THE BEST ITS SPECIES HAS DEVELOPED IN
THOUSANDS OF YEARS OF EVOLUTION: AN INFALLIBLE
INSTINCT, AN EXTRAORDINARY CAPACITY TO LEARN
FROM EXPERIENCE, AND A BODY THAT IS PERFECTLY

Introduction

ADAPTED TO ITS ENVIRONMENT. THESE CHARACTERIS-
TICS MAKE THE YOUNG CREATURE MUCH MORE THAN A
SPLENDID EXAMPLE OF TENDERNESS AND CLUMSINESS.
IT IS A MARVELOUS ANIMAL, ENDOWED WITH EX-
TRAORDINARY POTENTIAL: SOON IT WILL BE ABLE FLY,
PREY, RUN AND SWIM LIKE NO HUMAN HAS EVER BEEN
ABLE TO DO. IT WILL DOMINATE ITS HABITAT AND GET
TO KNOW EVERY ONE OF ITS MYSTERIES, AND WILL
STRUGGLE TO SURVIVE, ARMED WITH MONTHS OR
YEARS OF APPRENTICESHIP UNDER THE TUTELAGE OF
ITS PARENTS OR OTHER MEMBERS OF ITS FAMILY OR
GROUP. LASTLY, IT WILL REPRODUCE AND TEACH ITS
YOUNG THE SECRETS OF ITS PRECIOUS GENETIC HER-
ITAGE. THESE ARE THE REASONS WHY BABY ANIMALS

Introduction

HAVE SO MUCH POTENTIAL AND WHY WE CAN LEARN SO MUCH FROM THEM.

THIS BOOK, INCLUDING THE SPLENDID IMAGES OF THE EVERYDAY EXISTENCE OF HUNDREDS OF SPECIES OF ANIMALS THAT ILLUSTRATE THEIR BEHAVIOR AS WELL AS TRULY POETIC MOMENTS IN THEIR LIVES, BRINGS TO LIFE THE ADVENTURE OF CHILDHOOD, WITH ITS CHAL-LENGES AND ACHIEVEMENTS, SO THAT YOU CAN DIS-COVER THROUGH THE EYES OF THE ANIMALS THE COM-PLEXITY, DEMANDS AND SHEER FASCINATION OF THE PATH NATURE HAS TAKEN TO POPULATE OUR PLANET.

25 ● East Africa. A young elephant trying to get in contact with its mother.

26-27 ● Asia. Duckling following their mother.

28-29 ● United States. Calves in a livestock farm.

30-31 ● Western United States. A 'summit meeting' between a chick and a toad.

FIRST STEPS

- Sub-Saharan Africa. This giraffe, born after a 15-month pregnancy, is being cared for by its mother.

INTRODUCTION First Steps

Weighing no more than a pound, almost without a coat, blind and with weak legs, the future lord of the arctic is virtually unrecognizable. When the long winter shadows finally give way to the great first day of spring, the polar bear cub will take its first unsteady steps outside the den and move toward the arctic sea. Finally, after months without eating, the mother can resume her life as a predator, and a taste of seal meat will be enough to make her cubs dream of becoming adults.

The young wildebeest, on the other hand, is born in the vast expanse of grass of the african savanna, a habitat where, for an herbivore, a

INTRODUCTION First Steps

SECOND'S HESITATION USUALLY MEANS CERTAIN DEATH. IN FACT, ALL THE PREGNANT FEMALE GNUS SYNCHRONIZE THEIR BIRTH IN ORDER TO REDUCE THE HERD'S PERIOD OF VULNERABILITY TO THE UTMOST. FOR THE BABY GNU THERE IS NO TIME FOR TENDER CARE: A VIGOROUS LICK TO RID IT OF ITS PLACENTA AND FETAL RESIDUE, FIVE MINUTES TO LEARN TO STAND STRAIGHT UP, AND ONE DAY TO ACQUIRE RUNNING SPEED ALMOST EQUAL TO THAT OF THE ADULTS.

OTHER YOUNG ANIMALS ARE EVEN LESS FORTUNATE. WHEN THEY ARE BORN THEIR PARENTS ARE ALREADY FAR AWAY, AND MAY HAVE EVEN FORGOTTEN THOSE EGGS LAID DURING THE FRENZY OF REPRODUCTION. SUCH IS THE CASE WITH THE HUNDREDS OF TINY SEA

First Steps
Introduction

TURTLES BORN ON SANDY BEACHES: AFTER STRUGGLING TO BREAK THEIR SHELL AND EMERGING WITH DIFFICULTY, THEY PLOD LABORIOUSLY TOWARD THE SEA WITHOUT ANY PROTECTION, EXPOSING THEMSELVES TO THE RAPTORS THAT FEAST ON THEM, OVERJOYED FOR SUCH AN ABUNDANCE OF FOOD. THIS IS THE TRAGIC BUT NECESSARY LAW OF NATURAL SELECTION THAT IS AT WORK ALREADY WHEN THE YOUNG ARE TAKING THEIR FIRST STEPS AND THAT SPARES VERY FEW FORTUNATE SPECIES: A DESTINY THAT MAY APPEAR CRUEL WHEN VIEWED BY COMPASSIONATE HUMANS, BUT IS REALLY THE MOST EFFICIENT INSTRUMENT AT THE SERVICE OF LIFE.

- Africa. A mother antelope prods her newborn baby with its snout.

United States. This least tern chick, which weights less than five grams, moves toward its mother.

40 • Europe. This wild goose chick will learn to fly in about five months.

40-41 • Europe. A very young Egyptian goose making clumsy attempts at flying.

42-43 • Sub-Antarctic area. This one-month-old penguin is almost ready to leave its nest.

44 and 45 ● Africa. Nile crocodile eggs hatch at the approach of the rainy season.

46-47 ● Africa. The first look at the world: baby crocodiles are able to live on their own after they are one month old.

West Africa. Newborn turtles on
a beach in the Dhalak Islands rush
to seek safety in the sea.

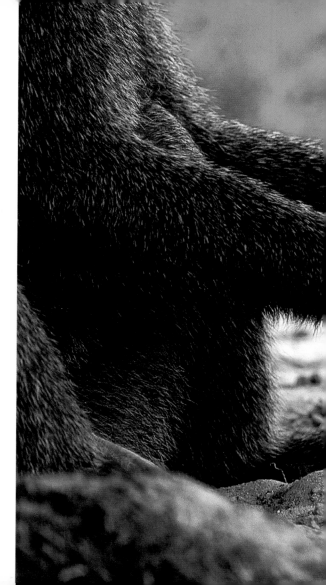

Africa. Exploring and playing in order to grow and develop properly is as essential to baboons as it is to humans.

66 Animals born in the savanna haven't much time to learn to use their legs to save their lives. Young gnus, like other prairie herbivores, are protected by the herd when they are born, but they can also count on their instinct and their mothers' encouragement to manage. 99

• East Africa. Fifteen minutes of struggling and vain attempts, and the baby wildebeest will be able to walk by itself.

54-55 ● East Africa. A baby
wildebeest takes its first steps
while its mother encourages it
with her snout.

55 ● East Africa. The newborn
wildebeest, followed by its mother,
is safe in the middle of the herd.

56-57 ● Central United States. A baby bison with its eyes still closed is touched by its mother.

58-59 ● Central United States. A newborn bison weighs 20-25 kilograms (44 to 55 lbs), while its mother weighs 450-500 (990-1100).

● East Africa. Once the amniotic fluid has been cleansed off, the newborn zebra will have white and brown stripes, the latter lighter those of its mother.

Africa. A mother Thomson's gazelle constantly follows her foal, which is still wet and tousled.

Africa. Baby elephants may be clumsy, but they are good and determined learners.

United States. Its long, thin legs help the colt to move around quickly with the herd few minutes after its birth.

68 and 69 ● Asia and Europe. Similar behavior patterns: a sheep and a cow use their snouts to push up their newborn.

70-71 ● United States. The first postpartum cleansing of calves in the Midwest prairies.

FAMILY LIFE

• Africa. Family life among cheetahs is concentrated in the two years
the cubs live with their mothers.

INTRODUCTION Family Life

SHELTER, WARMTH, CARE AND NURSING, FEEDING, AND IN A CERTAIN SENSE, TENDERNESS. WHEREAS FOR A BABY ANIMAL THE OUTSIDE WORLD REPRESENTS CURIOUS THINGS, FEAR AND ADVENTUROUS DISCOVERY, ITS FAMILY MEANS SURVIVAL AND LIFE, AND EACH SPECIES HAS DEVELOPED EFFICIENT SOLUTIONS IN ORDER TO GUARANTEE THIS. IN ELEPHANT HERDS, FOR EXAMPLE, WHEN THE MOTHER ELEPHANT HAS COME TO THE END OF HER 22-MONTH PREGNANCY, ALL THE OTHER FEMALES HUDDLE AROUND HER. LIKE EXPERT MIDWIVES THEY CARESS HER AND HELP HER DURING HER LABOR, PROVIDING HER WITH PRECIOUS MOMENTS OF REST JUST AFTER THE BIRTH, AS THEY THEMSELVES SEE TO THE IMMEDIATE NEEDS OF THE NEWBORN BY REMOVING THE PLACENTA, GIVING IT A

INTRODUCTION Family Life

SAND-BATH AND THEN HELPING IT GET ONTO ITS FEET. FROM THIS TIME ON THE BABY WILL RECEIVE ALL KINDS OF SPECIAL ATTENTION: IT WILL PLAY WITH THE OTHER YOUNG IN THE MIDDLE OF THE HERD, PROTECTED BY THE HUGE MASS OF THE ADULTS THAT RESEMBLES A LIVING CLOISTER, AND WILL LEARN SECRETS ON HOW TO LIVE A LONG, HAPPY LIFE. AS MORE COMPLEX BEHAVIORAL PATTERNS DEVELOP, THE PARENTS SPEND MUCH MORE TIME, EFFORT AND EN-ERGY IN LOOKING AFTER THEIR FEW YOUNG IN ORDER TO INCREASE THE PROBABILITY OF SURVIVAL. FROM THE MOST ANCIENT MICROORGANISM TO THE MOST HIGHLY EVOLVED ANIMAL, SURVIVAL IS GIVEN THE UTMOST PRIORITY, AND THE ANIMAL SPECIES ARE THEREFORE GIFTED WITH INCREDIBLE VARIETY. THIS IS THE CASE WITH MOST INVERTEBRATES, FISH

Family Life
Introduction

AND AMPHIBIANS. WHEN THE FEMALE FROG LAYS A MASS OF 10,000 EGGS, SHE IS CERTAINLY NOT THINKING OF RAISING AN EQUAL NUMBER OF YOUNG. ON THE CONTRARY, EXHAUSTED AFTER PRODUCING AND LAYING SO MANY EGGS, SHE SHOWS NO INTEREST IN THEM, LEAVING THEM TO THEIR FATE. WHAT WITH THE VORACITY OF PREDATORS, CHANGES IN CLIMATE, THE PRECARIOUSNESS OF THE MARSHY ENVIRONMENT AND THE UNCERTAINTY OF GENETIC MUTATION, ONLY A FEW HUNDRED TADPOLES WILL BE FORTUNATE ENOUGH TO SEE THE LIGHT OF DAY. FURTHERMORE, CANNIBALISM IS COMMON. BUT WHAT MATTERS IS THAT THE AIM OF PERPETUATING THE SPECIES HAS BEEN ACHIEVED.

77 ● Africa. Among zebras, the longest lasting relationship is the one between mothers and their young.

78-79 ● Antarctica. Penguins have strong family ties. Here a mother leads her young.

Antarctica. The baby penguin seeks warmth between the feet of its parents.

82 ● Antarctica. The 'family language' among penguins consists of certain calls and behavior patterns.

83 ● Antarctica. The penguin parents take turns caring for their young.

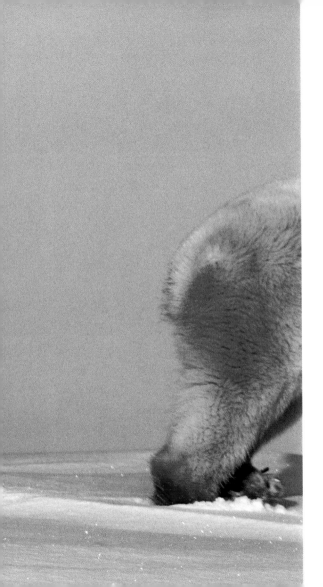

North America.
Between March and April
the young polar bears
can follow their mother
out of the den. Mother
and cubs will stay
together for two and a-
half years, while her
relationship with her
mate lasts no more than
a week.

North America.
The young Greenland
seal's family consists only
of its mother.

" Oceans ARE SO VAST THAT THEY CONCEAL MUCH MORE DANGER THAN THE LAND. HOWEVER, MERELY BEING THE GIANTS OF THIS UNDERWATER WORLD IS NOT ENOUGH TO SURVIVE IN THE DEPTHS OF OUR GLOBE: IT IS NECESSARY TO DEPEND ON THE FAMILY, THE GROUP, AND THE UNITY OF ITS MEMBERS. "

• Antarctica. Two killer whales emerge from the school. These mammals spend all their life in family groups of 5-20 individuals.

North America. Young
killer whales learn from
the other members of
the group by staying
close to them.

Atlantic Ocean. Each group of killer whales has its own 'language' of special sounds, as well as those common to the entire species.

● Atlantic Ocean.
There are strong social
bonds among bottlenose
dolphin families, which
consist of 5-10
members.

96-97 ● Pacific Ocean. The adult humpback whale's maneuvers are imitated by its calf.

97 ● Pacific Ocean. Family relationships in the groups of humpback whales are regulated by the most complex 'language' in the marine world.

● Pacific Ocean. Among humpback whales, only the relation between the mother and her young lasts for a relatively long time.

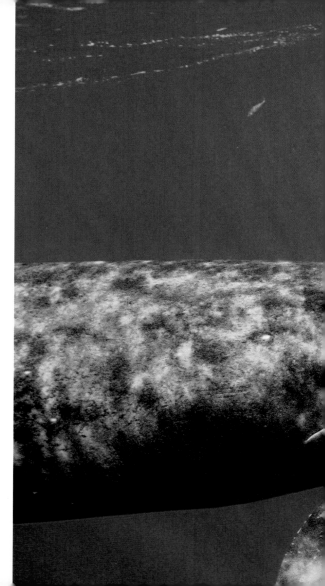

● Pacific Ocean. Humpback whales can often be seen in couples consisting of the mother and calf, sometimes escorted by a male.

102-103 ● Pacific Ocean. By swimming near its mother, the young dolphin learns to coordinate its breathing rhythm with hers.

104-105 ● Africa. The female Nile crocodile uses her jaws as a convenient way to transports her young.

" THE MOTHERS OF THE ANIMAL KINGDOM ARE ALWAYS READY TO SACRIFICE THEMSELVES FOR THEIR YOUNG, PROVIDING SECURITY AND EDUCATION. THERE IS NO TENDERNESS IN THE WORLD OF NATURE, BUT THE FAMILY OFFERS SENSE EVEN TO THIS DIFFICULT AND CRUEL EXISTENCE. "

● East Asia. The young Japanese macaques are reared mostly by their mothers, but the males also help.

108 ● Africa. Chimpanzees always maintain strong relationships with their mothers, even when they are fully grown.

109 ● South Asia. A show of affection between mother and child orangutan.

IN ORDER TO COMMUNICATE, MAMMALS USE VAR-
IOUS MEANS THAT MAN HAS LOST IN THE COURSE OF TIME.
THE 'KISS,' PHYSICAL CONTACT AND OTHER PHYSICAL
RELATIONS ARE SPONTANEOUS OR INSTINCTIVE MANIFES-
TATIONS THAT ARE NOT BURDENED BY THE WEIGHTY
MEANING OUR CULTURE IMPARTS.

● South Asia and Africa. Orangutans and giraffes: the former live
separately for the most part, while the latter form variable small
groups in which all the mothers together care for the young,

112 ● Africa. Female kobs form maternal groups that include the young and one adult male.

113 ● Africa. The groups of impala stick together, but there is little interaction among the members, except for the relationship between mothers and their young.

Africa. Elephant herds are dominated by the females and headed by a matriarch.

116, 117 and 118-119 ● East Africa. The herd provided protection and at the same time teaches social behavior to the young elephants, which are rarely separated from the females.

120-121 ● Africa. Mother leopard playing with her cub: this is the family.

122 and 123 ● Africa. Lionesses are very fond of their young and, if conditions are favorable, are first-rate mothers.

124-125, 126-127 ● Africa. Lions are sociable creatures; in fact, they are the only true cats that live in rather large groups.

128-129 and 130-131
Africa. Lionesses are
very scrupulous about
educating their cubs and
consume a lot of energy
in doing so.

Africa. When the lion cubs are still too small to do much by themselves, their mother has to move them from one lair to another.

Africa. This young cheetah will live with its mother for about a year and a half.

Africa. This is a lucky family: such a large litter of cheetahs is the result of excellent environmental conditions.

Africa. In order to rear her young, the mother cheetah must have a lot of patience and be constantly attentive.

● Central Europe. The mother lynx and her cub make up the family, which stays together
until the young creature has learned all the secrets of hunting and survival.

142, 143 and 144-145 ● Africa. All this anger on the part of the adults only means that they are tired of being pestered by their young.

Africa. Family fun: a young female plays with her little brother.

United States. Mother bear seems to be scolding her cub. In fact, reprimands are an important part of education among animals.

150-151 ● United States.
A red fox barks at a cub.

152-153 ● United States.
When a wolf cub breaks
the rules of the pack it is
immediately punished.

Atlantic Ocean. This small sea lion is being severely reprimanded.

• Africa. Female hippopotamuses spend many hours in water, forming family groups of 10-20 members (and sometimes as many as 100) during the day, while they spend the night alone with their young.

Africa. Contact with their parent is reassuring for both the young chimp and cheetah.

• North Asia and Northwestern United States. Bear cubs follow the example of their formidable mother to prepare themselves for the dangerous life ahead.

United States. A climbing lesson for a brown bear cub and a puma only a few weeks old.

● Africa. The male leopard sometimes helps the female to rear the cubs.

166 ● Australia. Female koalas give birth to cubs that weigh 60 grams and must rear them without any help from their mates.

167 ● United States. Young opossums climbing on their mother's body.

Africa. Both male and female ostriches are very protective of their chicks and can become quite ferocious if the family is threatened.

170-171 ● Africa. Zebra family groups are very close-knit, even during the terrible seasonal migrations, when they move together with thousands of wildebeests.

172-173 ● Africa. This young giraffe follows its galloping mother. The females of this species live together with their only child in their own territory, far from the males.

" BISONS ARE RATHER COMPETITIVE: THE MALES FIGHT TO CONQUER THE FEMALES, AND THESE LATTER FIGHT IN ORDER TO HAVE THE BEST GRAZING LAND. NATURALLY, THE YOUNG DO NOT PARTICIPATE IN THE ADULTS' AGGRESSIVE BEHAVIOR, BUT THIS 'PACIFISM' LASTS ONLY UNTIL THEY ARE GROWN ENOUGH TO COMPETE WITH THEIR PARENTS. "

• United States. Young bisons, whose coat is still reddish, are reared by the females, who live apart from the males.

" SMALL EYES THAT ARE NOT YET ABLE TO TOLERATE LIGHT: YOUNG ANIMALS ARE BORN BLIND AND SLOWLY MOVE INTO THE LIGHT. IN FACT THEY ARE BLIND TWICE OVER, BECAUSE AT THE BEGINNING OF THEIR LIFE THEY KNOW NOTHING. HOWEVER, THEIR PERIOD OF DARKNESS IS ILLUMI-NATED BY CERTAIN INEXPLICABLE, IMPALPABLE FLASHES OF INSTINCTIVE BEHAVIOR. "

• United States. A young porcupine uses its sense of smell to 'study' its mother. The porcupine families consist of a monogamous couple and a single-birth cub.

Europe. Olfactory communication is also essential for baby marmots in order to get to know and to recognize their parents.

" THE PRAIRIE IS TOO VAST TO BE TAKEN IN BY THE UNCERTAIN SIGHT OF YOUNG ANIMALS THAT MUST STILL GROW. THUS, EVERY NEARBY, COLORED AND MOVING OBJECT IS A DISCOVERY AND AN INVITATION TO EXPLORATION, BUT IF THE MOTHER IS CLOSE BY YOU CAN BE SURE THAT THE YOUNG CREATURE WILL SOON FORGET IT AND GO TO HER. "

• Northern United States. Both mother and father wolf are always patient with their young, and in fact are exemplary parents.

Northwestern United States. A red fox cub tries to prolong its mother's loving attention.

● Eastern United States. For the Canadian lynx, the only social unit consists of the mother and its cubs, with an average of two per birth.

● Asia and United States. Protection of the young is the primary motive of the bonds among animals that are not sociable and that are consequently easy prey, such as Bengal tigers and American bears.

188-189 ● North America. Canadian geese stay with their mate and their families for their entire lives.

190-191 ● North America. A young Canadian goose seeks protection in its parent's feathers.

192-193 ● North America. The mother seems irritated by her child's clumsiness, but she is really encouraging it.

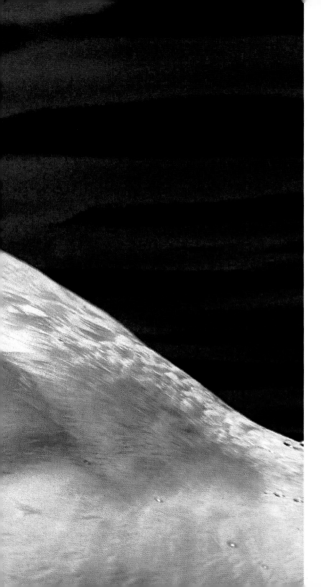

● Northern Europe.
Black-necked swan
and mute swan chicks
swimming.

" **F**RAGILE AND HELPLESS THOUGH THEY BE, YOUNG DUCKLINGS AND OTHER CHICKS CAN COUNT ON THEIR TIRELESS PARENTS. THE LATTER – IN SOME CASES BOTH MALE AND FEMALE – DO EVERYTHING THEY CAN TO PROVIDE FOOD FOR THEIR YOUNG, CONSUMING A GREAT DEAL OF ENERGY IN DOING SO, AND ALSO DEFEND THEM WITH AMAZING DETERMINATION. "

196 ● North America. This is the first swim for these young geese.

197 ● North America. For adult grebes, the best and safest way to look after their young is to take them along with them.

● Europe. A goose
extends a protective
wing over her brood.

Southwestern Atlantic Ocean. A black-browed albatross couple is observing its baby with love.

• South America. These two young frogs are safe on the adults' heads.

United States. A row of piglets following the mother. Pigs, even domestic ones, are gregarious and territorial, and the females form hierarchical groups with their respective young, while the males are solitary creatures.

PLAY And
TRICKS

• North Asia. A Siberian tiger and her cub having fun tussling in the snow....

INTRODUCTION Play and Tricks

Lion cubs attack their mother's tail the same way they will attack the gazelles that for the present they merely observe from a distance. By taking care of their small brothers, young female monkeys learn the ways of motherhood in advance. The young okapi learns the techniques of combat and the sense of being a dominating male from his father, who lets his son "beat" him by dealing blows with its long neck and throwing him to the ground. And human children play war games, perhaps too often... Just like humans, the most intellectually evolved creatures on the earth, young animals love to play more

INTRODUCTION Play and Tricks

THAN ANYTHING ELSE. FOR THAT MATTER, PLAY BOTH REQUIRES AND DEVELOPS A REPERTORY OF COMPLEX BEHAVIORAL PATTERNS INDISPENSABLE FOR THE GROWTH OF THE YOUNG. PLAY INVOLVES THEM IN THE MOST IMPORTANT FORMS OF THE LEARNING PROCESS. IN FACT, THE YOUNG ANIMAL THAT PLAYS IS PRACTICING ALL THOSE SKILLS THAT WILL MEAN THE DIFFERENCE BETWEEN LIFE AND DEATH WHEN IT IS AN ADULT: THE ABILITY TO OBTAIN PLENTIFUL SOURCES OF FOOD BY GATHERING OR HUNTING, TO ESCAPE QUICKLY FROM AN AMBUSH, TO FIGHT FOR DOMINANCE IN THE GROUP... BUT PLAY IS NOT ONLY A TRAINING GROUND FOR ADULT LIFE, AS CAN BE SEEN IN THE MAD BUCKS OF COLTS, THE ACROBATIC SOMERSAULTS OF YOUNG

Play and Tricks

Introduction

GIBBONS, AND THE APPARENTLY SENSELESS AND SUD-
DEN FLIGHT OF CHICKS OF MANY DIFFERENT SPECIES.
ANY PARENT KNOWS THAT ITS YOUNG HAVE A SUR-
PLUS OF ENERGY AND EXUBERANCE THAT MANIFESTS
ITSELF AS CURIOUS, HYPERACTIVE TENSION THAT CAN
BE PLACATED ONLY WHEN THE CREATURES ARE EX-
HAUSTED. PLAY IS THEREFORE BOTH A SORT OF SAFE-
TY VALVE FOR THE SPASMODIC AND EXPLOSIVE
CHANGES CONNECTED TO GROWTH AND A MEANS OF
SOUNDING OUT THE CONTINUOUSLY DEVELOPING PO-
TENTIAL AND LIMITS OF THE YOUNG ANIMALS: KNOWL-
EDGE AND AWARENESS THAT WILL BE MOST USEFUL IN
THE FUTURE....

● Africa. The tails of the prey are playthings for lion cubs.

212 ● United States. A brown bear cub plays with a feather of an American eagle.

213 ● East Africa. A lion cub plays by itself in the savanna.

● Africa. Playing is always useful: by chewing on and 'attacking' wood, leopard cubs sharpen their teeth and practise hunting techniques.

South Africa. The mother cheetah's tail is an irresistible attraction for its cub.

East Africa. Lionesses
are always patient
with their cubs.

East Africa. Playing with adults, lion cubs learn how to behave when they will be adult.

222 and 222-223 • East Africa.
A friendly tussle between lion clubs;
the elder one curbs its superior
strength.

224-225 and 226-227 •
East Africa. Young animals' play
foreshadows the behavior of adults
while hunting and fighting.

228-229 ● South America. Jaguar cubs play (rather roughly, it must be said) above all to keep active.

230-231 ● East Africa. An enthusiastic young cheetah uses elephant dung as a ball.

East Africa. Young cheetahs already reveal exceptional agility in their play and chases.

East Africa. Six month-old cheetahs chasing one another across the savanna.

● East Africa. Young cheetahs, with juvenile fur, play in the savanna.

238, 239 and 240-241 ● Europe. Posing and moving like fighters, these European brown bear cubs confront one another in the water.

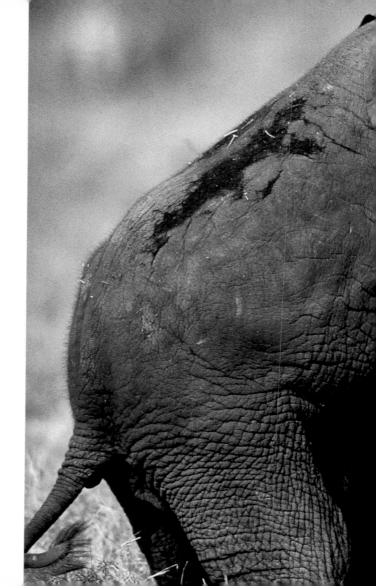

East Africa. The 'victor' and 'vanquished' in a mock fight.

244 ● Southern Africa. A scuffle between young elephants of different ages, probably one- or two-year-olds.

245 ● Southern Africa. By playing with their trunks, young elephants learn to use it.

" LIKE HUMAN BEINGS, ANIMALS, ESPECIALLY YOUNG ONES, NEED TO PLAY IN ORDER TO LEARN TECHNIQUES AND SOCIAL BEHAVIOR. THEREFORE, DEPRIVING THESE CREATURES OF THEIR PLAY IS TANTAMOUNT TO DEPRIVING THEM OF A VERY IMPORTANT PART OF THEIR LEARNING PROCESS AND MAKING THEM EVEN MORE VULNERABLE. "

• South Asia. Roughhousing among young Bengal tigers

● Asia. These young Siberian tigers are playing in order to test their strength.

250 ● Asia. Young mongooses devote their energy to a playful struggle.

251 ● Europe. These red fox cubs refine their combat strategies through play.

" **M**AMMALS IN GENERAL, AND NOT ONLY YOUNG ONES, LIKE PLAYFUL COMBAT. YOUNG CANINES SUCH AS WOLF AND FOX CUBS IMITATE THE 'SERIOUS' BEHAVIOR OF THE ADULTS AND AT THE SAME TIME LEARN THE RULES OF THE PACK HIERARCHY, WHICH ARE INDISPENSABLE FOR SURVIVAL. "

252 ● United States. Play is preparation for hunting for red fox cubs.

253 ● North America. Gray wolf puppies playing, learn how to attack a prey.

254 ● North America. Young wolves from the conifer forests of the Northwest play together.

255 ● United States. Two wolf cubs tussling in front of their den.

United States.
These two young
prairie dogs are for sure
having fun.

Eastern Europe. The combat between Eurasian lynx cubs occurs in a spirit of play, but they are sometimes wounded, especially in the eye.

260 • Southeast Asia. A young orangutan uses a liana to swing over the water.

261 • Southeast Asia. A very young orangutan skillfully balancing itself.

262 • East Africa. An adult with young chimpanzees, whose play is very 'human'.

263 • East Africa. These chimps' tenderness and expressions reveal evident relations with human behavior.

Africa. Two young
baboons playing near
the Luangwa River,
in Zambia, while the
group is resting.

South Asia. Young langurs 'dancing' while playing in the sun.

● East Asia. Two young Japanese macaques playing with snowballs, something they learned from humans.

● East Asia. Young Japanese macaques play only with a few select friends and not with all the peers in the group.

272 ● North America. Rolling in the snow is great fun for polar bear cubs, as well a for the adults.

273 ● United States. This polar bear cub is toying with a whalebone.

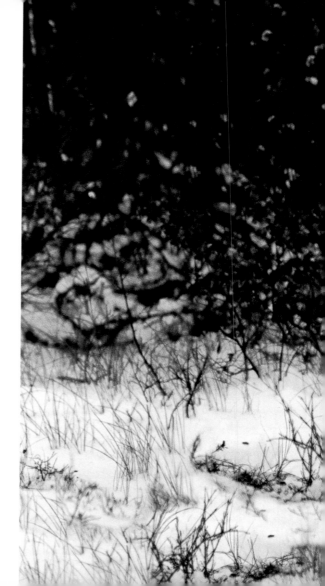

274-275 ● North America. A polar bear cub playing with a twig.

276-277 ● North America. Three month-old polar bear cubs run in the snow.

278 ● South America. By chasing one another in play, young guanacos improve their agility.

279 ● Africa. The young also have fun by frightening other animals.

● Europe. Colts at play: here again this is a prelude to adult combat.

282-283 ● Europe.
This one year-old colt
is playing vigorously.

284-285 ● Europe.
West Highland white
terrier puppies.

286-287 and 288-289 ●
Europe. A samoyed and
golden retriever. If there is
only one stick, the young
creatures' play is even
more fun.

290 • Europe. Golden retrievers: a stick is an everlasting 'bone of contention.'

291 • Europe. Two griffon pups face one another.

292-293 ● Europe.
Attack and display
behavior on the part of
two domestic kittens.

294-295 ● Europe.
A kitten's leap is not only
play, but serves as
training for future
hunting.

A DANGEROUS WORLD

South Asia. A young orangutan seems frightened by the violence of the rainstorm.

INTRODUCTION A Dangerous World

INFANCY IS A KIND OF STEEPLECHASE IN WHICH ONLY A SMALL NUMBER OF CONTENDERS WILL MANAGE TO ARRIVE AT THE FINISHING LINE. YOUNG ANIMALS ARE CONSIDERED TASTY TIDBITS FOR MOST OF THE CREATURES THEY COME ACROSS, SO THEY MUST QUICKLY LEARN HOW TO RECOGNIZE DANGER, COPE WITH FEAR, AND COME UP WITH EFFICIENT DEFENSE STRATEGIES.

WHEN TORMENTED BY ITS OWNER'S ROUGH CARESSES, A PUPPY ROLLS ONTO ITS BACK. THIS ACT OF UNCONDITIONAL SURRENDER CAN BE INTERPRETED AS A MEANS OF IMPLORING PITY AS WELL AS EXPRESSING TOTAL FAITH IN ITS ADVERSARY'S SENSE OF FAIR PLAY – A BEHAVIORAL PATTERN INHERITED DIRECTLY FROM

INTRODUCTION A Dangerous World

WOLVES, THE ANCESTORS OF DOGS. FOR MANY YOUNG CREATURES SALVATION LIES PRECISELY IN THEIR SMALL SIZE, AND ALTHOUGH THEIR SHORT LEGS MAKE A HASTY RETREAT IMPOSSIBLE, THEY CAN TRY TO BE "INVISIBLE" BY STANDING PERFECTLY STILL, PERHAPS WITH THE HELP OF MIMETIC COLORING, WHICH IS A VERY COMMON AND FLAWLESS STRATEGY THAT NATURE HAS PROVIDED, ESPECIALLY WHEN THE ANIMAL IS TERROR-STRICKEN. THE GREATEST FEAR FOR A YOUNG ANIMAL IS BEING WITHOUT ITS MOTHER. MOST SPECIES HAVE SPECIAL SOUNDS THAT MOTHERS AND THEIR YOUNG EMIT TO LOCATE ONE ANOTHER, A SORT OF SECRET LANGUAGE THAT IS PERCEIVED BEFORE ANY OTHER SIGNAL AND THAT BREAKS THE MOTHERS'

A Dangerous World

Introduction

OR YOUNG ANIMALS' HEART WHEN NO REPLY IS HEARD. DANGER MAY TAKE ON MANY DIFFERENT FORMS. IT IS OFTEN CAUSED BY THAT IRREPRESSIBLE CURIOSITY THAT DRIVES THE YOUNG CREATURES TO START EXPLORING THEIR SURROUNDINGS. AND PAIN IS THE RESPONSE TO A RECKLESS ACT OR WRONG MOVEMENT: THE BLACK BEAR CUB GROANING IN PAIN BECAUSE OF THE THORNS IN ITS NOSE WILL NOW UNDERSTAND FOR THE REST OF ITS LIFE WHAT TERRIBLE DEFENSIVE WEAPONS A PORCUPINE HAS; AND THE FOX CUB SPITTING STICKY SLIME FROM ITS MOUTH WILL LONG REMEMBER THE DISGUSTING TASTE OF TOADS...

301 ● Europe. Porcupines are dangerous, as this young German shepherd has discovered.

302-303 ● Africa. For this young kob thirst could be fatal.

East Asia. With their frightened look, these young macaques seem to be expressing a great need for protection.

306-307 ● Africa. Dog-faced baboons fleeing a predator, carrying their babies on their backs.

308-309 ● East Africa. A group of lycaons attacks a female wildebeest and her calf

310-311 ● Africa. The arrival of an eagle terrorizes two Thomson's gazelles.

312-313 ● Africa. A black-backed jackal faces a baby wildebeest.

314-315 ● Africa. This young antelope shows no fear, evidently because the cheetah is tired and cannot manage to catch it.

316-317 ● Africa. Antelope and cheetah: the final spurt.

Australia. A baby kangaroo, even if already grown, hides in its mother's pouch, its favorite refuge.

320 ● Europe. For this red fox cub in its lair there are many potential dangers.

321 ● Europe. A long-eared owl chick swells its plumage to frighten predators.

● Europe. Kittens are born hunters, but they run away in a jiffy as soon as their 'prey' gets tired of them.

LITTLE
CLOWNS

- Africa. Lion cubs mimic the expressions of adults, generally after having noted a pungent odor.

INTRODUCTION Little Clowns

The large, wide-open eyes are situated under the median line, since the cranium is often roundish. The snout is chubby and flat, and the limbs and tail are short with respect to the body. A thick layer of fat and soft, bushy hair make most baby animals look somewhat like a powder puff. All of them, especially birds and mammals, tend to look alike; despite the fact that they belong to different species, they share many physical features. But their appearance is not everything. What makes these hairy or feathery dolls so tender and joyful is the face they make – comical or serious – while concentrating on a seemingly

INTRODUCTION Little Clowns

UNIMPORTANT DETAIL: A BLADE OF GRASS, A TINY IN-
SECT, A FLY BUZZING OVERHEAD, THE PLAY OF LIGHT
ON WATER OR UNDER THE WATER....

THESE EXPRESSIONS BECOME EVEN MORE CHARAC-
TERISTIC THROUGH THE SOUND OF THE VOICE, WHICH
IS SHARPER AND HIGHER THAN THAT OF THE ADULTS
BECAUSE HIGH SOUNDS ARE EASIER TO HEAR AND LO-
CATE, AND THROUGH THE BIZARRE, CLUMSY MOVE-
MENTS THAT IN ADULTHOOD WILL BE REPLACED BY A
MORE DIGNIFIED CARRIAGE: HEAD BUTTS TO ATTRACT
ATTENTION, CAPERS MADE TOWARD A DESIRED OB-
JECT, EXAGGERATED CALLS TO MAKE AN INSIGNIFI-
CANT REQUEST. THE FACIAL EXPRESSIONS OF YOUNG
ANIMALS ARE MESSAGES THAT THEIR WORLD TRANS-

Little Clowns
Introduction

MITS TO THE ADULT WORLD: ETHOLOGISTS HAVE NOT-ED THAT THESE SIGNALS HAVE THE MAGIC POWER OF CHECKING THE AGGRESSIVE BEHAVIOR OF AN ADULT. THEY MAY NOT WORK WITH A HUNGRY PREDATOR, BUT THEY USUALLY SAVE THE YOUNG FROM THE ANGER OF THE DOMINANT MALE AND, PRECISELY BECAUSE THEY ARE UNIVERSAL SIGNALS, THEY SOMETIMES HELP AN ORPHAN TO BE ADOPTED BY A NEW MOTHER, WHO MAY NOT NECESSARILY BE OF THE SAME SPECIES. THESE MESSAGES ARE EXTREMELY EFFICACIOUS, AS CAN BE SEEN BY THE FEELING OF TENDERNESS AND FONDNESS PRODUCED IN READERS BY THE PHOTO-GRAPHS IN THIS BOOK....

329 • United States. A little long-eared owl 'winks' from its tree shelter.

330-331 • Europe. Two calves pose together for the photographer.

332-333 ● United States. An amusing grizzly cub leans against a Ponderosa pine.

333 ● United States. A young wildcat tries to climb a trunk

334-335 ● United States. When they are two months old, wolves try to howl.

Northeastern United States and Asia. Much stronger and more aggressive than the kittens they seem to be, a red lynx cub and a tiger cub hissing in a threatening manner.

● East Africa. This young
chimpanzee is resting
safely among the foliage.

● Africa. Chimpanzees are particularly likeable and charming animals: whether they are alone or in company, they always provide us with a laugh.

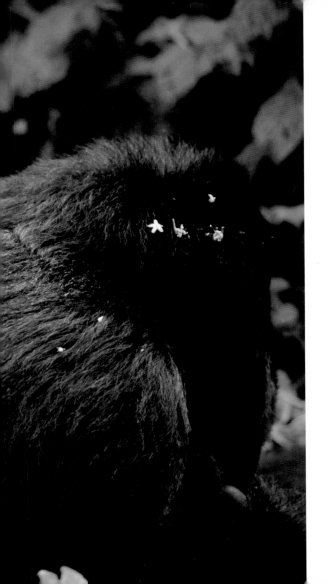

Africa. A young mountain gorilla travels in comfort on an adult's back.

344-345 ● South Asia. There's a mischievous look in this young orangutan's eyes!

345 and 346-347 ● South Asia. Sheer pleasure and absolute rest are on the agenda for these two young orangutans.

● South Asia. A young orangutan takes refuge from the rain, using a large bough as an umbrella.

• East Asia. This young giant panda seems to be smiling while at play.

● East Asia. These snowflakes are like confetti for the young giant panda, which is having fun tossing them quickly into the air.

Europe. These beagle puppies' looks perfectly express the absolutely inoffensive nature of this species.

" YOUNG ANIMALS HAVE WHAT WE CONSIDER AMUSING BEHAVIOR BECAUSE THEY LACK EXPERIENCE AND TEND TO MAKE A MESS OF THINGS. BUT THERE IS SOMETHING MORE SUBTLE AT WORK HERE: WHATEVER THEY DO, THEY STIR TENDERNESS IN THE OBSERVER, WHICH SERVES TO PROTECT THEM. "

• Europe and North America. The young gray seal and polar bear cub seem to be dodging the photographer's lens.

358, 359 and 360-361 ● Europe. It is difficult not to consider these young seals' "affected" behavior as 'human'.

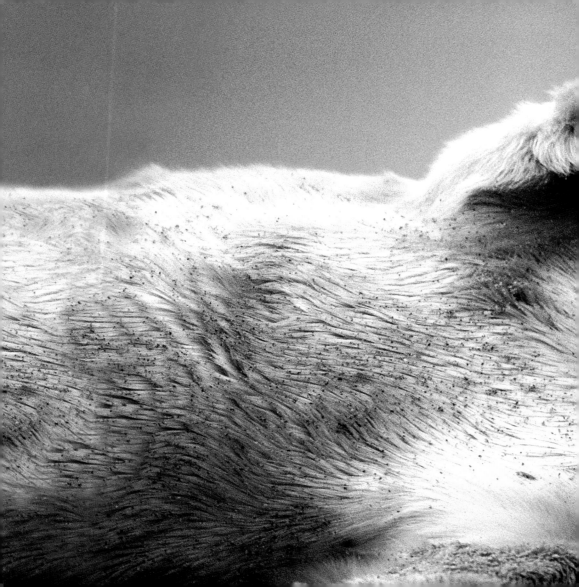

BEING A YOUNG ANIMAL MEANS MAKING THE FIRST CHOICES. THESE ARE SIMPLE CHOICES, BUT CONSUME ALL THE ENERGY OF THE CREATURES MAKING THEIR 'DEBUT' IN THE WORLD. EVEN BY THEMSELVES THEY CAN PERFECT THEIR POTENTIAL AND CAPACITIES BY USING THE SIGNS THAT NATURAL INSTINCT HAS PROVIDED THEM WITH.

362 • United States. A four month-old grizzly bear is 'cleaning' its fur.

363 • Africa. A baboon engaged in grooming.

Europe. A wildcat enjoys blissful rest in the midst of Nature.

366 ● Western United States. This young grizzly is trying to snatch insects.

366-367 ● Eastern United States. A young clouded leopard prepares to seize an insect.

368 • Africa. A young giraffe photographed during mastication.

369 • Africa. The seven vertebrae on this young Masai giraffe's long neck will allow for its bizarre growth.

Africa. These amusing expressions are really connected to the animals' perception of and reaction to pheromones.

372-373 ● Africa. Lion cubs participate emotionally in the life of the pride.

374-375 ● Africa. Young leopards with their rather weak roars try to capture their mother's attention.

376 ● Africa. A young cheetah completes its yawn by sticking out its tongue.

377 ● Africa. A penetrating odor triggers a characteristic reaction on the part of this young cheetah.

378 and 379 ● United States. Young lynxes hissing and mewing.

380-381 ● Central Europe. This young island pony neighs to communicate with other ponies.
In fact, neighing is a rather articulated 'language.'

382 ● United States. An American Saddlebred colt neighs while following its mother.

383 ● Central Europe. An Arabian thoroughbred is partly covered by its mother's tail.

Central United States. This grizzly cub jumping in the water is obviously quite pleased.

United States. This brown bear cub seems to be wheedling to attract the photographer's attention.

Africa and United States. The leaps of these cubs – a cheetah and a bear only
a few months old – express all the vitality of youth.

Central Australia. A red kangaroo cub seeks protection in its mother's pouch.

East Africa.
An African elephant only
a few weeks old tries to
drink with its small trunk.

394 ● Central-south Asia. A young Asian elephant has just finished wading in the water.

395 ● East Africa. This young elephant will need a lot of time and experience to learn to use its trunk properly. The trunk is its means of communication and expression, as well as its external breathing organ and auxiliary 'arm.'

Africa. A young elephant having trouble drinking.

398 and 399 • Africa. Young elephants often seek, in every way, physical contact with the female adults of the herd and with their playfellows.

400-401 • Asia. In the eyes of these Bengal tiger cubs a fallen tree trunk looks like an insurmountable obstacle.

402 • United States. A grizzly cub encounters a wild gramineous plant.

403 • United States. The red fox cub will never sate its hunger but it will certainly give free rein to its desire for play.

Europe. A young common raccoon swinging acrobatically.

United States. With their unmistakable coats, these young skunks seem to be posing for a photo.

South America. Twin births are common among tamarins and these two young look really identical.

● West Indian Region.
A Sifaka or prosimian,
carries its five month-old
baby on its back.

● Western United States. Communication between cubs: the two brown and black bears exchange clear signs of affection with the utmost spontaneity.

414 • East Africa. The young crocodile learns the tricks of mimicry.

415 • East Africa. These two Nile crocodiles seem to be confronting one another.

416 ● Africa. A newly hatched cattle egret has an insatiable appetite.

417 ● Southeastern United States. Two purple herons that seem to be following the latest fashion in hairdos.

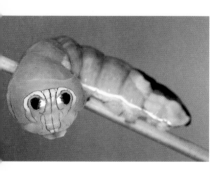

418 ● Europe. The 'eyes' at the end and along the body of certain chrysalides look like the snout of larger animals in order to frighten predators.

418-419 ● Europe. The 'muzzle' of this chrysalis looks like gaping jaws.

WARM And SAFE

United States. A young raccoon peeps out of its den.

INTRODUCTION Warm and Safe

THE WORDS "LAIR," "DEN" AND "NEST" EVOKE THE MOST ANCIENT REFUGE, THE NATURAL CONTINUATION OF THE PRENATAL EXPERIENCE. THE LAIR, DEN OR NEST IS THE PLACE THAT MEANS WARMTH, THE FIRST SENSORY EXPERIENCES, THE FIRST APPROACH TO FAMILY RELATIONS. IT ENSURES SAFETY, LOVE, AND COMFORT, EVEN WHEN IT IS A DARK AND DAMP CAVE, A CREVICE BETWEEN ROCKS BEATEN BY THE WIND. SOME YOUNG ARE BORN IN A HOLE IN THE GROUND SO SOFT, DARK AND WARM THAT IT IS LIKE BEING IN THEIR MOTHER'S WOMB AGAIN. SOME WIN THEIR FIRST BATTLE BY FINALLY BREAKING THROUGH THEIR SHELLS AND FIND THEMSELVES IN A LOVINGLY PREPARED NEST LINED WITH SOFT FEATHERS ON THE MOST INACCESSI-

BLE FORK OF A HIGH TREE. AND THERE ARE SOME WHO ARE DESTINED TO HAVE A MORE ADVENTUROUS BIRTH. THE LAIR OF THE BABY BAT, FOR EXAMPLE, IS A COMFORTLESS, DARK AND DEEP CAVE THAT IS ENCRUSTED WITH SALTPETER AND OTHER MINERAL DEPOSITS AND IS VERY COLD, SINCE THE SUN NEVER SHINES THERE. THE MOTHER GIVES BIRTH AT A DIZZYING HEIGHT WHILE HANGING UPSIDE DOWN FROM THE VAULT. WITH ITS STRONG CLAWS DESPERATELY CLUTCHING ITS MOTHER'S SKIN AND ITS LIPS ON HER NIPPLE, THE BABY BAT BEGINS ITS BIZARRE CAREER AS A FLYING MAMMAL. AT HIGH LATITUDES CONTINUOUSLY LASHED BY A BITTERLY COLD WIND, POLAR BEARS FIND SHELTER IN THE UNUSUAL WARMTH OF A LAIR DUG OUT OF THE ICE. IT IS

Warm and Safe
Introduction

HERE THAT THE CUBS ARE BORN, SPEND THEIR FIRST WEEKS OF EXISTENCE AND, THANKS TO A HIGH-CALORIE MILK DIET, PREPARE TO COPE WITH THEIR HOSTILE ENVIRONMENT. THE LAIR MAY BE THE CLOSEST THING TO THE MOTHER'S WOMB, BUT THE DREAM OF EVERY YOUNG ANIMAL IS CERTAINLY THE REFUGE USED BY MARSUPIALS: THE SOFT, VELVETY POUCH HEATED BY THE MOTHER'S BODY, LINED WITH HER TEATS HEAVY WITH MILK AND OFFERING THE REASSURING RHYTHM OF HER HEARTBEAT... BABY KANGAROOS ALSO TAKE REFUGE THERE WHEN IN DIFFICULTY, EVEN WHEN THEY ARE ADOLESCENTS AND MANAGE TO STICK ONLY THEIR HEADS INSIDE.

• Australia. Young wallabies stay in their mother's pouch for 9-10 months and are weaned when they are around 17 months old.

Europe.
The red fox litters
are prudently kept
near the lair.

Europe. Roe deer
choose sheltered woods
or reed beds in humid
areas to rest in.

430 • Europe. A young rodent comes out of its lair.

431 • Europe. In its tree shelter a young marten is safe from all its predators.

United States.
A five-month old puma
plays near its lair under
a rock, with its mother
nearby.

434-435 and 435 ● Northern United States. Lynxes have their dens among rocks or bushes, as well as in hollow tree trunks.

436-437 ● North America. Mother bear makes her cubs come out of their shelter in the snow.

North America.
A Greenland seal less
than a week old in
its shelter.

● Central United States.
A large group of prairie
dogs on the lookout at
their den.

442-443 • East Africa. A litter of lion cubs has found its lair under a large dead euphorbia.

444-445 • United States. A young coyote squeezes into the lair while its brother waits for its turn.

446-447 • Central Asia. The lairs of the rare snow leopard or irbis are crevices situated in inaccessible sites.

● North America. The den of young raccoons usually consists of a hollow tree, which they emerge from one month after birth.

450 ● Northeastern United States. Wood duck chicks leave the nest a short time after hatching.

451 ● South America. The austral conure (parakeet) builds its nest in crevices and hollow tree trunks about 2 to 3 meters (6.5 to 10 ft) from the ground.

● Europe. European wildcats
  peeping out of their lair.

454 ● United States. The mother wolf leaves her babies in the den while she goes out to hunt for food.

454-455 ● United States. Coyote cubs live in the den for about a year and then go off on their own for good.

South Asia.
Tigers prefer luxuriant
vegetation for their dens.

458-459 ● Africa.
The cattle egret builds
its nest on a vast
platform of branches,
on large trees.

460-461 ● Eastern
Europe. The whiskered
tern nests on beds of
floating vegetation.

Southwest Atlantic Ocean. The black-browed albatross uses stones, grass and rubble to build its nest on rocky islets

464 ● Pacific Ocean. The locations of seabirds' nests are among the most vertiginous in nature.

465 ● Pacific Ocean. This young gannet in its nest is complaining because it is hungry.

466 ● United States. A brood of long-eared owls observing from the nest.

467 ● Southwest United States. The tall, thorny and very sturdy saguaro cacti are excellent places for nesting for the great horned owl.

468 and 469 ● Northeast United States. A long-eared owl maneuvering in its retreat.

470-471 ● Mediterranean area. A falcon chick shrieking at the entrance of its nest on a rock face.

PRIMARY NEEDS

East Africa. In its eagerness, this lion cub is suckling in an unusual and rather precarious position.

INTRODUCTION Primary Needs

THE SIGNAL MAY BE A HOWL, A CRY, INSISTENT CHEEPING, OR REPEATED MOVEMENTS OF THE HEAD. IT SPREADS THROUGH THE AIR, AMONG THE BRANCHES OF THE FOREST, ON THE PRECIPITOUS CRAGS OVERLOOKING THE SEA, IN THE SAVANNAS, AND IN THE DEPTHS OF THE OCEAN, UNTIL IT REACHES AN EAR OR EYE THAT IS ABLE TO DISTINGUISH IT FROM A MILLION OTHERS. THIS IS THE CALL OF A YOUNG, HUNGRY ANIMAL, HEARD BY ITS PARENTS, WHO, DRIVEN BY INELUCTABLE INSTINCT, IMMEDIATELY COME TO ITS AID. IT IS A POWERFUL NATURAL ALARM, AN INSTRUMENT THAT THE IRONCLAD LAWS OF NATURE HAVE PROVIDED FOR YOUNG ANIMALS, WHICH WOULD OTHERWISE SURELY DIE.

INTRODUCTION Primary Needs

WHOLLY DEPENDENT ON THEIR PARENTS FOR A PERIOD THAT RANGES FROM A FEW MINUTES TO A FEW YEARS, ACCORDING TO THE SPECIES, THE YOUNG ARE LIKE SPONGES THAT ABSORB AN AMAZINGLY LARGE AMOUNT OF FOOD: IF FROM BIRTH THE WEIGHT OF A HUMAN CHILD DOUBLES IN ABOUT SIX AND A HALF MONTHS, THE YOUNG BLUE WHALE, THE LARGEST LIVING MAMMAL IN THE WORLD, INCREASES ITS WEIGHT MORE THAN SEVEN-FOLD IN THE SAME SPACE OF TIME. THE SECRET LIES IN THE MILK, THE BEST NOURISHMENT FOR MAMMALS, WHICH IN MOST CASES IS PROVIDED BY THE MAMMARY GLANDS OR IS TRANSUDED, AS OCCURS WITH THE MONOTREMES. THESE LATTER ARE THE MOST PRIMITIVE MAMMALS, WHICH LAY EGGS

Primary Needs
Introduction

AND HAVE NO NIPPLES ON THEIR BREASTS. CONSEQUENTLY, THE BABY DUCK-BILLED PLATYPUS HAS TO HURRY TO LICK THE MILK EXUDING IN TINY DROPS FROM ITS MOTHER'S ABDOMEN.

HOWEVER, NOT ALL THESE CREATURES ARE LUCKY ENOUGH TO HAVE SPECIAL FOOD PROVIDED BY A PARENT; IN FACT, THE DIET OF MOST YOUNG ANIMALS IS SIMILAR TO THAT OF THE ADULTS, WITH THE DIFFERENCE THAT THE FORMER ARE NOT ABLE TO OBTAIN ENOUGH FOOD BY THEMSELVES. THEREFORE, THE RELATIONSHIP BETWEEN PARENTS AND CHILDREN IS VERY CLOSE FOR MOST OF EARLY CHILDHOOD, THE YOUNG TOTALLY RELYING ON THEIR MOTHERS AND FATHERS, WHICH SOMETIMES CREATES STRONG LIFE-

Primary Needs
Introduction

LONG BONDS. THE SPECIAL HELP AFFORDED BY THE PARENTS, WHICH CONSUMES A LOT OF THEIR ENERGY, CONSISTS OF LEAVING WORMS, GAME, FISH OR SEEDS IN THE NESTS OR LAIRS, WHERE THE ADULTS CAN TAKE A SHORT REST BEFORE SETTING OFF IN SEARCH OF MORE FOOD. OR THE NOURISHMENT MAY BE A FRESH-LY KILLED GAZELLE, STILL WARM AND COVERED WITH BLOOD, LEFT FOR THE VORACIOUS JAWS OF LION CUBS. OR IT MAY BE A PILE OF DUNG THAT THE TINY DUNG BEETLES – ALWAYS HUNGRY AND INSATIABLE, LIKE ALL OTHER YOUNG ANIMALS – WILL DEVOUR IN A FEW MINUTES.

478-479 ● East Africa. Young elephants suckle for two years or even more, though some plants are added to their diet after the first five months.

480 ● Northwestern United States. Brown bear cubs trying to catch a salmon, which is a real treat.

481 ● Northwestern United States. This ten-month-old grizzly seems to be undecided as to whether it should continue playing with the salmon or begin eating it.

Africa. A young lycaon eats while the adult keeps watch.

Africa. Cheetah cubs
devouring a prey.

486 ● Europa. A red fox
cub confronting
a lamb's paw.

486-487 ● East Africa. For this
young lion, a zebra's paw is more
a plaything than food.

● Africa and United States. The lion and puma cubs are having their first taste of meat.

" WITH THEIR APPETITE, VORACIOUS CREATURES DETERMINE THE EQUILIBRIUM OF A WORLD THAT FEEDS ON ITSELF. HUNGER DISTURBS THE TRANQUILITY OF ORGANISMS, PROVIDING THEM WITH STIMULI AND COURAGE; IT DRIVES YOUNG ANIMALS TO ESCAPE FROM DEATH BY DEMANDING FOOD AND ADULTS TO ENTER THE BATTLE FOR SURVIVAL WITH DETERMINATION. AND THUS LIFE CONTINUES. "

490 ● Europe. Two young wolves devouring a hare that was killed by an adult.

491 ● Europe. A red fox cub 'begging' for part of the prey.

North America and northwestern United States. Two young seals put their noses near the freezing water.

Southern Africa. A young kob at the watering hole while an adult keeps careful watch.

496 • United States. While it is drinking, a young roe deer is intrigued by its reflection in the water.

497 • United States. Like all mammals, red fox cubs can resist thirst for only a short time.

North America. Mother wolf escorts her cub to the water hole.

500 and 501 • Asia. Two female orangutans with their young beside them are using their 'hands' as cups.

502-503, 504-505 and 506-507 • Africa and Central Australia. One week-old warthogs, red kangaroos and lion cubs, all alert, are drinking together with the adults, which are protecting them.

● East Africa. One of the things a lion cub has to learn is how to drink properly.

East Africa. The swamp is relatively safe from predators, but the mother will not abandon her child while drinking.

● Southern Africa. A young
elephant can drink up to 20 liters
(5.5 gallons) of water a day, either
with its trunk or mouth.

"WATER AND FOOD ALMOST MONOPOLIZE THE LIFE CYCLES. AND YET, ONCE THEY HAVE ARRIVED AT A RIVER, HAVE SEIZED THEIR PREY OR HAVE EATEN THE BEST GRASS, THE SINISTER LIGHT OF THE STRUGGLE FOR SURVIVAL DIES OUT AND IS REPLACED BY THE JOY OF HAVING WON THE BATTLE ONCE AGAIN. "

• East Africa. A memorable watering place for a young elephant that is deep in the swamp waters.

516 and 517 ● Africa and United States.
These lion and lynx cubs are too busy
suckling to bother about anything else.

518-519 ● East Africa. The patient lioness
lies on her back with a tangle of cubs on
her stomach.

East Africa. When they are two months old, young rhinos suck their mother's milk every 2-3 hours for about three minutes.

522 ● Africa. The little time that young impalas are with their mothers is spent suckling.

523 ● Africa. This young elephant is looking for its mother's teats under her front legs.

524-525 ● Africa. Young zebras feed on their mothers' milk until they are 13 months old.

526 ● Africa. The digestive system of baby giraffes develops their ten months of breast-feeding.

527 ● Africa. As they grow, young sassabies find it harder to gain access to their mothers' teats.

Europe. A young horse drinks 10-13 liters of milk per day.

530 ● Europe. The 'artificial' weaning of farm-bred calves lasts from one to two weeks.

531 ● Europe. The milk suckled during the first few days after birth (colostrum) increases the lambs' immunity.

Africa and Asia. Anthropomorphic primates (in this case, baboons and orangutans) suckle their young 'upon request' several dozen times per day.

● East Asia. Young giant pandas are quite greedy when suckling and protest with unexpectedly loud noises when they are pushed away from their mother's teats.

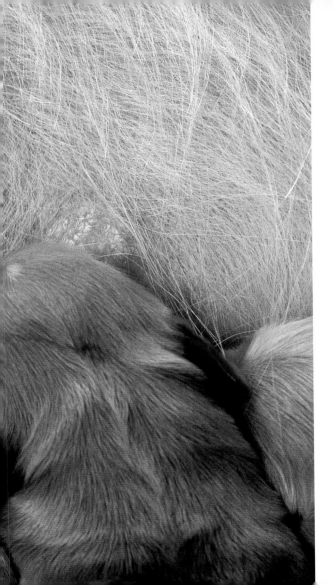

536-537 ● Europe. These three-day-old golden retriever puppies devote all their energy to feeding.

538-539 ● Europe. Young boars that still have streaked coats crowd together to drink their mothers' milk.

Europe. A whiskered tern and an Arctic tern caring for their young. With time, the parents' efforts at feeding their chicks become more and more difficult and time-consuming.

542-543 ● East Pacific Ocean. A lesser frigate feeds its young.

543 ● Europe. Both parents are busy feeding their young among the reed beds.

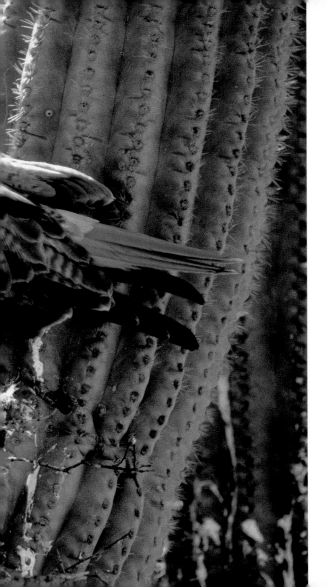

544-545 ● Southwest United States. A red-tailed hawk regurgitating its food in its nest among the cacti.

546-547 ● South America. The adult hummingbird gives its tiny chick insects that feed on nectar.

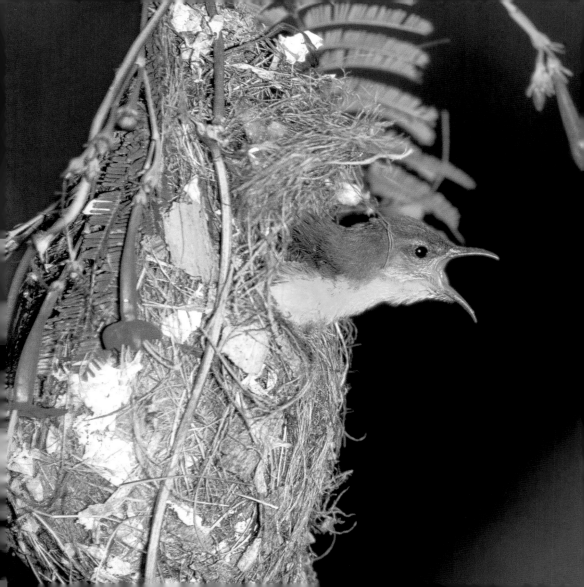

North America. Tiny but quite visible in their nests, these wren and welcome swallow chicks are screaming for food.

• Antarctica. A young emperor penguin's principal food is rich in krill.

EXPLORING The WORLD

• Africa. This young cheetah is in a curious observation position.

INTRODUCTION Exploring the World

IN THE NEST THE MOTHER HAS DUG WITH SUCH LOVING CARE AND COVERED WITH EARTH, ROTTING LEAVES AND DUNG, MORE THAN 50 EGGS ARE IN THE LAST STAGE OF THEIR GROWTH, WHILE THE PARENTS KEEP CONSTANT GUARD. ABOUT THREE MONTHS AFTER BEING LAID, THE EGGS ARE READY TO HATCH. AS SOON AS THEY ARE BORN, THE BABY CROCODILES ARE EXTREMELY CURIOUS: EVERYTHING THAT MOVES ATTRACTS THE ATTENTION OF THEIR SLIT EYES. IT IS CRUCIAL FOR THEM TO RECOGNIZE THEIR MOTHER – IN WHOSE MOUTH THEY CAN TAKE SHELTER FOR ANOTHER COUPLE OF MONTHS – FROM OTHER JAWS SIMILAR BUT MUCH MORE LETHAL. THE TINY CROCODILES MUST STILL LEARN TO HUNT IN AMBUSH, BUT ALREADY THEY INSTINCTIVELY BE-

COME IMMOBILE AT THE SLIGHTEST STRANGE SOUND. A QUICK ESTIMATION OF THE SIZE OF THE "INTRUDER" IS ALL THEY NEED TO DECIDE WHETHER TO TRY TO EAT IT OR ESCAPE IN ORDER NOT TO BE EATEN. ALL THINGS CONSIDERED, THE LIFE OF A CROCODILE DOES NOT ENTAIL DIFFICULT DECISIONS.... THE BEHAVIOR OF MANY ANIMALS IS RIGIDLY DETERMINED BY IMMUTABLE CODES INHERITED FROM INNUMERABLE GENERATIONS, WITHOUT ANY POSSIBILITY OF FREE CHOICE. THIS IS THE CASE WITH BEES AND THEIR COMPLICATED DANCE. ON THE OTHER HAND, THE BEHAVIOR OF MAMMALS, BIRDS AND MANY OTHER MORE EVOLVED ANIMALS IS THE FRUIT OF AN ONGOING LEARNING PROCESS, WHICH CAN BE MODIFIED BY THE CREATURES' OWN EXPERIENCE AND THAT OF OTHERS

Exploring the World
Introduction

AND WHICH IS MEDIATED BY CURIOSITY. HERE NATURE HAS PROVIDED THEM WITH AN EXPEDIENT: THE STIMULUS TO BECOME ACQUAINTED WITH THE OUTSIDE WORLD IS AFFORDED BY THE PLAYFUL DESIRE TO EXPLORE, WHICH MANIFESTS ITSELF AS THE ENERGETIC, IRREPRESSIBLE PERPETUAL MOVEMENT SO TYPICAL OF YOUNG ANIMALS. THUS, THE URGE TO DISCOVER THE SURROUNDINGS IS STIMULATED BY INSTINCT, BUT THE YOUNG CREATURES' PARENTS, WHICH ARE SUCH LOVING AND INFLEXIBLE TEACHERS, ALSO PLAY AN IMPORTANT ROLE. IT TAKES YOUNG ELEPHANTS SIX YEARS TO USE THEIR TRUNK, AN ORGAN WITH EXCEPTIONAL POTENTIAL THAT THEY CANNOT USE AT ALL AT BIRTH, WHILE AT THE END OF THIS

Exploring the World
Introduction

LONG APPRENTICESHIP THE TRUNK IS USED TO EAT, DRINK, COMMUNICATE, WASH, FIGHT AND COURT. YOUNG CHIMPANZEES LEARN TO USE BRANCHES TO SCOOP TASTY TERMITES OUT OF ROTTING STUMPS, A SOURCE OF FOOD UNKNOWN TO MOST OTHER ANIMALS. KITTENS LEARN HOW TO HUNT FROM THEIR MOTHERS. BLACKCAP CHICKS SEEM TO BE ONLY ASKING FOR FOOD WITH THEIR OPEN BEAKS, BUT THEY ARE REALLY CAREFULLY MEMORIZING THE SOUNDS EMITTED BY THEIR PARENTS; IN FACT, BLACKCAPS FROM DIFFERENT ZONES CHIRP WITH DIFFERENT INFLECTIONS, AND THOSE THAT HAVE NOT LEARNED THEIR OWN LANGUAGE ARE CONSIDERED INTRUDERS AND ARE TREATED AS SUCH.

558-559 ● United States. For a lynx cub even a dry leaf is potential prey.

Europe. With its thin, agile body and dark coat that is hard to see against the background, this young otter is ready to explore the surroundings.

Africa. A one-year-old lion cub observing a tortoise shell.

" THE MORE DIFFICULT AND STRANGE THE OBJECT OF THEIR EXPLORATION, THE MORE IT STIRS THE CURIOSITY OF CUBS. AS FOR YOUNG FELINES, BESIDES THEIR UTTER PERSISTENCE, THEY SEEM TO MANIFEST A 'PHYSIOGNO-MIC' CURIOSITY AND EVEN AMAZEMENT WHEN ENCOUN-TERING SINGULAR CREATURES SUCH AS A TORTOISE. "

564 ● Africa. A leopard tests the patience of a tortoise.

565 ● Central America. This young ocelot will observe the tortoise for quite some time.

South Africa. A canebrake frog finds itself in a dangerous confrontation with a young crocodile.

• Asia. Curiosity is discovery. At the slightest noise, two tiger cubs, one of which is an albino, leave off their play.

● East Africa. Though
they are rather good
swimmers, young zebras
must learn to be wary in
the African rivers, which
are infested with
crocodiles.

572 and 573 ● South Asia. After their first swims, the Bengal tiger cubs are quite at their ease in water, more so than other felines.

574-575 ● Eastern United States. Clouded leopards exploring a tree trunk run aground.

East Africa. Cheetah and lion cubs learn by watching the adults while safely hidden by tree trunks, grass or rocks.

United States. Lynx cubs exploring mysterious crevices. Their curiosity is as great as their prudence.

Eastern United States.
Bear cubs are good
climbers and soon learn
to climb up conifers.

Africa. Flying insects attract the attention of a young cat.

Europe. Since they have to learn from experience "in the field," kittens are usually more active that grown cats.

586 ● Africa. Learning to climb up trees, which are usually safe refuges in the savanna, will be quite useful in adulte life.

587 ● United States. A puma, or mountain lion, cub climb a tree paying great attention.

North America. These Canadian
lynx and bobcat cubs seem
almost ready to jump on a prey.

East Africa. A "new" animal attracts the attention of a young elephant.

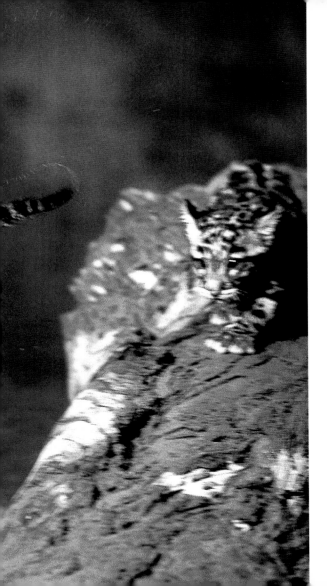

592-593 ● United States. A clouded leopard cub avoids the water. Another one, at right, is waiting for his turn.

594-595 ● Africa. A lion cub solves the problem of fording with a leap.

Western United States. A coyote cub carefully examines a primrose.

Europe. A hare less than seven months old tests his sense of smell.

600 ● South Asia. Ants and their eating habits attract the attention of a young orangutan.

600-601 ● United States. Nectar is a delicious discovery for this brown bear cub.

United States.
This brown bear
cub's exploration has
become risky.

United States. For young bobcats all prospects are interesting.

• United States. Plants, which are staples in their diet, are more than interesting for brown bear cubs.

608-609 ● Africa. This baboon just over a month old is examining dry grass.

610-611 ● East Africa. During his excursion of discovery, a lion cub has found a nest.

United States. Ducklings putting the "rapids" of a stream to the test.

Europe. A swallowtail
butterfly inadvertently
attracts the attention
of a young lynx.

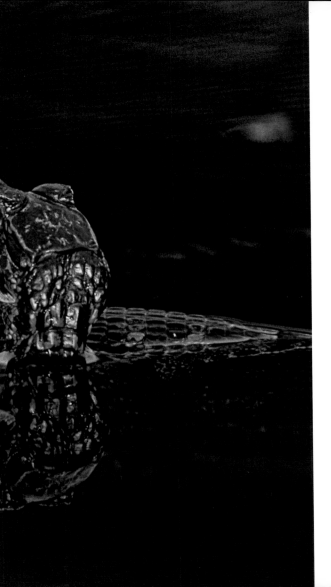

South America. Caiman chicks are not dangerous for one year and hardly ever venture out of their nests.

618 • Southeastern Pacific Region. A kitten ventures into the tropical vegetation.

619 • United States. The extremely vulnerable young wolf faces the outside world prudently.

● Europe. This brown bear cub is so intent on seeing a crow from up close that he is not afraid of the void.

Europe. Kittens 'playing' with prey might be a sign of their innate need to hunt.

624 • Europe. For this golden retriever, the fence is a border to be crossed.

625 • Europe. Kittens, like many other felines, prefer elevated places to observe things.

BECOMING SELF-SUFFICIENT

East Africa. Still a bit clumsy, this young elephant is throwing dust on its body to get rid of insects.

INTRODUCTION Becoming Self-Sufficient

Every sound and flash of light causes apprehension in a newborn animal, which still remembers and yearns for the warmth of its mother's womb, but that same baby will soon make astoundingly fast progress in its drive to attain the freedom of adult life. Young monkeys strongly feel the "call of the wild" and wander far from their mothers to explore trees and distant areas. Besides being risky, this impatience is not altogether justified, because being a youngster has its advantages. The young male chamois is well aware of this: when overcome in combat by older, more experienced males, it resorts to infantile postures in order to mitigate

INTRODUCTION Becoming Self-Sufficient

ITS RIVAL'S AGGRESSIVENESS AND THUS AVOID PAINFUL WOUNDS. IN ANY CASE, FOR ALL YOUNG ANIMALS THERE COMES THE MOMENT WHEN THEIR MOTHERS VIGOR-OUSLY PREVENT THEM FROM REACHING THEIR NIPPLES – THE MOMENT WHEN INFANCY COMES TO AN END AND CHILDHOOD BEGINS, WITH ITS FEARS, TENSION AND UN-CERTAINTY. AT THIS POINT THE PERSONALITY OF THE YOUNG ANIMAL IS ALREADY FORMED, AND ITS SOCIAL ROLE AND PROBABILITY OF SURVIVING IN AN ENVIRON-MENT THAT HAS SUDDENLY BECOME CLEARLY HOSTILE, CAN BE SURMISED. FOR INSTANCE, MALE LION CUBS (UNLIKE THEIR SISTERS, WHICH ARE WELCOME IN THE FAMILY TERRITORY) ARE FORCED TO ABANDON THEIR GROUP AND EXPERIENCE THE HUMILIATION, AS WELL AS

Becoming Self-Sufficient
Introduction

HUNGER, RESULTING FROM THE INEVITABLE FAILURE OF THEIR FIRST ATTEMPTS AT HUNTING. THE SAME IS TRUE IN THE ANDES, WHERE THE ADULT GUANACOS DRIVE AWAY WITH BITES THE SAME YOUNG MALES THAT A FEW DAYS EARLIER WERE CONSIDERED THE PRIDE AND JOY OF THE HERD. IN THE VOYAGE TOWARD MATURITY THERE ARE THOSE THAT RUN AND THOSE THAT HESITATE. BUT THE PATH GOES IN ONE DIRECTION ONLY AND INEVITABLY PASSES THROUGH A DRAMATIC MOMENT: THE FIRST FLIGHT FROM DIZZYING HEIGHTS FOR THE YOUNG EAGLE, THE FIRST DIVE INTO FREEZING WATER FOR THE YOUNG PENGUIN, THE FIRST PREY PURSUED AND KILLED, THE TASTE OF WARM BLOOD....

• Southwestern Atlantic Ocean. With time, the Adélie penguins' brown feathers gradually shed, disappearing completely when they are one year old.

"THE BORDERLINE GETS CLOSER EVERY DAY: BECOMING AN ADULT IS NO LESS TRAUMATIC THAN BIRTH. BUT THERE IS NO TIME TO WASTE, AS LIFE PRESSES FORWARD. THE YOUNG ANIMAL WILL HAVE TO LIVE IN SOLITUDE, YET ITS POTENTIAL HAS BEEN INCREASED BY ITS YOUTHFUL VIGOR."

632, 633 and 634-635 • Africa. Almost a full-fledged adult and able to hunt by itself, this cheetah is attacking a young gazelle.

636-637 • Africa. Once they have attained self-sufficiency in two years, these young lions must leave their pride and search for another one.

638-639 ● Africa.
The offensive tactics of
this lion cub is already
developed.

640-641 ● Africa.
This young lion feels
confident enough to
launch an audacious
attack against a young
elephant.

● Africa. For the young elephant, charging at the lion is more a game than a form of defense.

East Africa. Two young elephants are imitating the more serious combats they will have when they are adults.

● Europe. Two fallow deer in combat with their antlers locked.

648-649 ● Africa. Catching small prey without any help is the first important achievement for a growing lion cub.

650-651 ● United States. This young wolf, already a skillful hunter, returns home with rather large prey.

● Europe. This one-and-
a-half-month-old wolf cub
is trying to howl, but
manages only to produce
a high-pitched wail.

SLEEPY
HEADS

Canada. A young lynx dozes off with its head against its mother's body.

INTRODUCTION Sleepyheads

Soft but highly resistant silk sheets in which to sleep as a caterpillar and wake up as a butterfly: in many species of invertebrates the state of lethargy, which is necessary in order to arrive at the stage of adulthood, is protected by the warm walls of a cocoon. Many other mothers entrust their sleeping young to the protection afforded by their lairs or nests. After having consumed so much energy to build a safe and comfortable refuge for their young, the parents can now leave them alone for a few hours, and when they return they will see a maze of muzzles, snouts or beaks absorbed in deep sleep....

INTRODUCTION Sleepyheads

FOR YOUNG ANIMALS, SLEEP IS A PRECIOUS MEANS OF RECHARGING A SMALL VOLCANO WITH THE ENERGY IT HAS USED UP DURING THE DAY. DEPENDING ON THE SPECIES, THESE ARE MINUTES OR HOURS OF ABANDON AND DETACHMENT DURING WHICH THE PRESENCE OF THE PARENTS IS VIRTUALLY INDISPENSABLE. OFTEN THE SITE IS THE LAIR – A GROTTO, HOLE, OR CAVERN – BUT THIS IS NOT ALWAYS THE CASE. FOR EXAMPLE, THE YOUNG OF TREE-DWELLING SPECIES SLEEP ON BRANCHES IN THE MOST ABSURDLY PRECARIOUS POSITIONS. THE YOUNG SLOTH, THE KING OF SLEEPYHEADS, MANAGES TO REST PEACEFULLY WHILE LYING ON ITS MOTHER'S STOMACH, ITS TINY PAWS CLUTCHING HER COAT WHILE SHE MOVES ABOUT IN THE WOODS BY SWINGING FROM

Sleepyheads
Introduction

ONE BRANCH TO ANOTHER HIGH ABOVE THE GROUND. FOR THAT MATTER, THE NATURAL REFLEX WHEREBY A NEWBORN HUMAN FIRMLY GRASPS ANYTHING THAT TOUCHES THE PALM OF HIS/HER HAND IS NOTHING MORE OR LESS THAT A VESTIGE OF THAT REMOTE AGE WHEN OUR SPECIES HAD SIMILAR PROBLEMS.

THE CHOICE OF "PYJAMAS" MAY ALSO PLAY A CRUCIAL ROLE IN ENSURING PEACEFUL REST: THE SOFT DOWN ON THE CHICKS OF SEA BIRDS IS SO MIMETIC THAT THEY CAN SLEEP IN SAFETY WHILE THEIR PARENTS ARE AWAY FOR HOURS. AND CERTAINLY NO ONE WILL DISTURB THE SLEEP OF THE BABY CHAMELEON, WHICH IS PERFECTLY INVISIBLE EVEN DURING THE DAY.

- Northeastern America. A young Greenland seal rests on the snow, taking in the warm rays of the sun.

● East Africa and northern United States. A female cheetah and polar bear rest with their cubs, protecting them with their bodies.

Asia and East Africa. A Bengal tiger cub and a cheetah cub use fallen trunks as pillows.

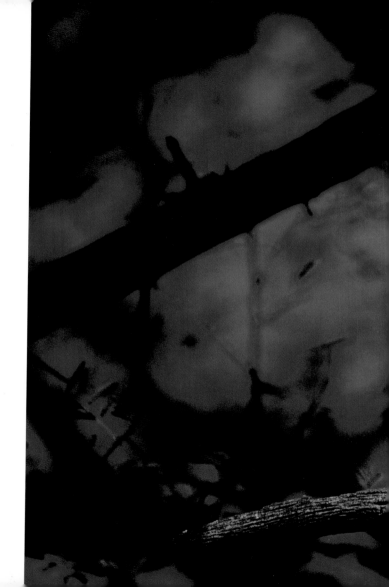

● South Asia. Toward evening, the barred jungle owls are about to wake up to begin their nocturnal hunting.

666 • East Africa. These cheetah cubs sleep in a circle in order to keep warm.

667 • Central United States. Inside a hollow trunk, three lynx cubs make up a cluster of fur.

" DESPITE WHAT THE HYPERACTIVE MEMBERS OF THE ANIMAL WORLD MIGHT THINK, SLEEPING IS TANTAMOUNT TO LIVING. SLEEP IS SO IMPORTANT THAT THE FACT THAT IT 'ROBS' THE CREATURES OF MUCH OF THEIR LIFE IS JUSTIFIED. YOUNG ANIMALS SLEEP OFTEN AND DREAM WITH INTENSITY, RECREATING THE EXPERIENCES OF THEIR EARLY LIFE IN KALEIDOSCOPIC FRAGMENTS. "

668 ● East Asia. Giant panda cubs sleep face to face.

669 and 670-671 ● Europe. These golden retrievers have also decided to take a refreshing nap.

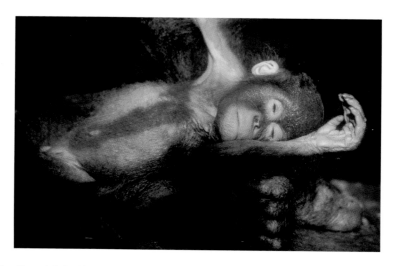

Southeast Asia. Young orangutans rest on their mothers' chests, which is "special treatment" that will last until another one is born.

674-675 ● United States. Any place and position will do for a nap for this black bear.

676-677 ● Europe. A solitary ball of fur, or better, a sleeping European brown bear.

678-679 ● Europe.
A loon chick sleeping on
the leaf of an aquatic
plant.

680-681 ● Europe.
The mother wild duck is
awake, while her brood
is still sleeping deeply.

682-683 ● Asia.
A young Shar-pei with
its wrinkled coat sleeps
deeply.

Europe. A dachshund puppy falls asleep on the cool grass of a lawn.

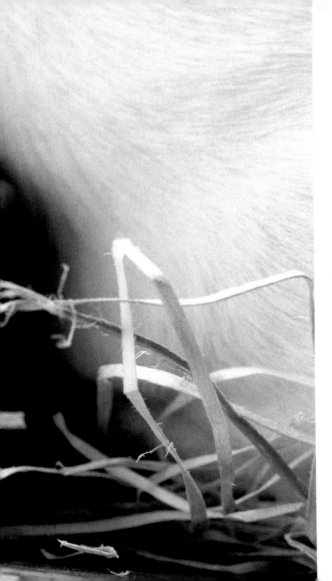

Europe. Puppies – in this case beagles – tend to sleep often during the day, especially after they have played.

Africa. These three young lycaons cuddle up while sleeping in order to stay warm.

Europe. While its young
is still asleep, a Eurasian
lynx stretches after resting.

Asia and Africa. Wide-open jaws and visible fangs: the yawning of tigers and lions is connected to the wakefulness-sleep transition and vice versa.

Africa. Head to head with her cub, this lioness will wake up immediately, if need be, to defend it.

696-697 ● North America. A polar bear shields its cub from the freezing wind with its body.

698-699 and 700-701 ● Australia. The imperturbable sleep of two seal calves close to their mother.

702-703 ● Northeastern America. Only two days old, this Greenland seal is able to sleep on the snow thanks to its thick fur and layer of fat.

North America. Two polar bears cuddled up to
their mother to stay warm while sleeping.

706 • Antarctic. Even in summer, emperor penguin chicks sleep with their beaks under their winds to avoid freezing.

707 • Antarctic. This young penguin is sleeping against its companion, also asleep.

● Europe. Kittens sleep a lot, especially during the day, and the total of REM (rapid eye movement, with dreams) sleep is three hours.

South Asia. A young Bengal tiger uses this tree trunk to sleep better.

• Europe and North America. Labrador puppy and a calf sleeping lightly.

"WHEN OBSERVING YOUNG ANIMALS WHILE THEY ARE SLEEPING, SOONER OR LATER WE AS CHILDREN REALIZE THAT THESE CREATURES ARE DREAMING – PERHAPS OF A RUN, A WHIMPER, A BLOW. WHAT IS INTERESTING IS THAT FOR THE FIRST TIME WE UNDERSTAND THAT THEY TOO HAVE A SOUL. "

714 • Europe. A domestic kitten sleeps next to its mother: cats, like all felines, are very scrupulous about seeing to the needs of their young.

715 • Asia. A Shiba Inu puppy. This is the oldest race of dogs in Japan.

716-717 ● Europe.
Wild piglets sleeping
in a forest.

718-719 ● Europe. During
the day, a forked tree is a
perfect bed for this young
tawny owl.

720-721 ● Central
America. A litter of
coypus about to
wake up.

● Domestic kittens spend most of the day dozing.

" UNBRIDLED YAWNS, POSITIONS THAT ARE IMPOSSIBLE TO ASSUME WHILE AWAKE, A TANGLE OF FUR THAT IS INSENSIBLE TO COLD. THE SLEEP OF YOUNG ANIMALS IS SPECTACULAR, ALMOST TO BE ENVIED, AND THE LITTLE CREATURES INDULGE IN IT WITH OBVIOUS PLEASURE, PARTLY BECAUSE IT IS USUALLY THEIR MOTHERS' HEARTBEAT THAT TICKS THE HOURS AWAY. "

● Europe. Kittens' sleep has 'active' phases, during which their muscle tone develops through movements and contractions.

Africa. While its mother
is moving with the group
in the wild game reserve,
the baby baboon sleeps
blissfully on her back.

INDEX

AUTHOR
Biography

ANGELA SERENA ILDOS

Angela Serena Ildos was born in 1967. She graduated in Natural Sciences at the University of Milan with a thesis on the environmental preferences of amphibians. Currently she works in a number of scientific fields; she is manager of the educational section of Milan's Natural History Civic Museum and is a lecturer in a number of cultural institutes, including the Università Popolare and the Libera Università Lombarda. She has published various books on nature and animals, and for Edizioni White Star she wrote and edited The Great National Parks of the World.

INDEX

PHOTO CREDITS

Page 1 T. Brakefield/Corbis/Contrasto
Pages 2-3 C. and M. Denis Huot
Pages 4-5 A. Maywald/Blickwinkel
Pages 6-7 K. Schafer/Hedgehog House
Pages 8-9 E. Janes/NHPA
Page 11 C. and M. Denis Huot
Page 13 S. Bloom Images/Alamy Images
Pages 14-15 S. Bloom Images/Alamy Images
Pages 16-17 N. Rosing/National Geographic Image Collection
Pages 18-19 J. Rotman
Page 21 D. J. Cox/Natural Exposures
Page 25 Ferrero Labat/Ardea
Pages 26-27 Gallo Images
Pages 28-29 E. Janes/NHPA
Pages 30-31 J. Habel/Corbis/Contrasto
Page 33 J. & A. Scott /NHPA
Page 37 T. Kitchin and V. Hurst
Pages 38-39 G.D. Lepp/Corbis/Contrasto
Page 40 G. Ziesler
Page 41 O. Broders/Blickwinkel
Pages 42-43 H. Garber
Page 44 I. Arndt
Page 45 I. Arndt
Pages 46-47 M. Harvey/Gallo Images/ Corbis/Contrasto
Pages 48-49 M. Bertinetti/Archivio White Star
Page 49 M. Bertinetti/Archivio White Star
Pages 50-51 K. Amman/nature Picture Library
Page 52 A. Shah/Nature Picture Library
Page 53 J. & A.Scott/NHPA
Pages 54-55 A. Shah/Nature Picture Library
Page 55 A. Shah/Nature Picture Library
Pages 56-57 Panda Photo
Pages 58-59 L. Kennedy/Corbis/Contrasto
Page 60 C. and M. Denis Huot

Pages 60-61 W. Wisniewski/Blickwinkel
Pages 62-63 C. and M. Denis Huot
Pages 64-65 A. Bannister/Gallo Images/ Corbis/Contrasto
Pages 66-67 L. Lenz/Blickwinkel
Page 67 L. Lenz/Blickwinkel
Page 68 L. Lenz/Blickwinkel
Page 69 S. Abell/National Geographic Image Collection
Pages 70-71 F. Grehan/National Geographic Image Collection
Page 73 Gallo Images/Corbis/Contrasto
Page 77 C. and M. Denis Huot
Pages 78-79 T. Davis/Corbis/Contrasto
Page 80 T. Davis/Corbis/Contrasto
Page 81 T. Davis/Corbis/Contrasto
Page 82 K. Schafer
Page 83 W.Khaeler/Corbis/Contrasto
Pages 84-85 N. Rosing/National Geographic Image Collection
Pages 86-87 N. Rosing/National Geographic Image Collection
Page 88 R.L. Pitman/Seapics
Page 89 R.L. Pitman/Seapics
Pages 90-91 B. Cole/Nature Picture Library
Page 92 A. Nachoum/Seapics
Page 93 G.Latz/Panda Photo
Pages 94-95 H. Schmidbauer/Blickwinkel
Pages 96-97 Ant Photo Library/NHPA
Page 97 A. Nachoum/Corbis/Contrasto
Pages 98-99 Marine Themes
Pages 100-101 J. Rotman
Pages 102-103 J. Rotman
Pages 104-105 J. Blair/Corbis/Contrasto
Page 106 T. Brakefield/Corbis/Contrasto
Page 107 T. Brakefield/Corbis/Contrasto
Page 108 Y. Forestier/Corbis Sygma/ Contrasto
Page 109 M. Bowler/NHPA

Page 110 Morales/Age Fotostock/Contrasto
Page 111 J. Jacobson/Associated Press
Page 112 A. & M. Shah
Page 113 C. and M. Denis Huot
Pages 114-115 S. Bloom/Alamy Images
Page 116 T. Davis/Corbis/Contrasto
Page 117 Blickwinkel
Pages 118-119 C. and M. Denis Huot
Pages 120-121 A. Shah/Nature Picture Library
Page 122 C. and M. Denis Huot
Page 123 C. and M. Denis Huot
Pages 124-125 S. Bloom/Alamy Images
Pages 126-127 C. and M. Denis Huot
Pages 128-129 C. and M. Denis Huot
Pages 130-131 C. and M. Denis Huot
Page 132 C. and M. Denis Huot
Page 133 C. and M. Denis Huot
Page 134 Nature Picture Library
Page 135 C. and M. Denis Huot
Pages 136-137 C. and M. Denis Huot
Page 138 C. and M. Denis Huot
Page 139 C. and M. Denis Huot
Page 140 M. Delpho/Blickwinkel
Page 141 C. Calosi
Page 142 C. and M. Denis Huot
Page 143 C. and M. Denis Huot
Pages 144-145 J. McDonald/Corbis/Contrasto
Pages 146-147 C. and M. Denis Huot
Pages 148-149 Bauer/Marka
Pages 150-151 D. Robert and L. Franz/Corbis/Contrasto
Pages 152-153 T. Kitchin and V. Hurst
Pages 154-155 Panda Photo
Page 156 A. and M. Shah/Hoaqui
Page 157 C. and M. Denis Huot
Page 158 K. Mosher/Danita Delimont Stock Photography

PHOTO CREDITS

PHOTO CREDITS

Page 585 O. Giel/Blickwinkel
Page 586 C. and M. Denis Huot
Page 587 T. Brakefield/Corbis/Contrasto
Page 588 A. Maywald/Blickwinkel
Pages 588-589 T. Brakefield/
Corbis/Contrasto
Pages 590-591 C. and M. Denis Huot
Pages 592-593 T. Brakefield/
Corbis/Contrasto
Pages 594-595 C. and M. Denis Huot
Pages 596-597 W.P. Conway/
Corbis/Contrasto
Pages 598-599 V. Munier
Page 600 A. & M. Shah
Pages 600-601 D.J. Cox/Natural Exposures
Pages 602-603 H. Garber
Page 604 D. Robert and L. Frantz/
Corbis/Contrasto
Page 605 D. Robert and L. Frantz/
Corbis/Contrasto
Page 606 S. Widstrand
Page 607 S. Widstrand
Pages 608-609 C. and M. Denis Huot
Pages 610-611 C. and M. Denis Huot
Page 612 H. Garber
Pages 612-613 H. Garber
Pages 614-615 R. Griffiths
Pages 616-617 T. Allofs/Corbis/Contrasto
Page 618 C. Monteath/Hedgehog house
Page 619 D. J. Cox/Natural Exposures
Pages 620-621 M. Delpho/Blickwinkel
Pages 622-623 J. Daniels/Ardea
Page 624 T. Davis/Corbis/Contrasto
Page 625 T. Davis/Corbis/Contrasto
Page 627 C. and M. Denis Huot
Page 631 W. Kaehler/Corbis/Contrasto
Page 632 C. and M. Denis Huot
Page 633 C. and M. Denis Huot
Pages 634-635 C. and M. Denis Huot
Pages 636-637 Alamy Images

Pages 638-639 C. and M. Denis Huot
Pages 640-641 A. Shah/Panda Photo
Pages 642-643 C. and M. Denis Huot
Pages 644-645 C. and M. Denis Huot
Pages 646-647 R. Tidman/Corbis/
Contrasto
Pages 648-649 C. and M. Denis Huot
Pages 650-651 T. Kitchin and V. Hurst
Pages 652-653 B.K Hubert/Panda Photo
Page 655 T. Vailo/Panda Photo
Page 659 N. Rosing/National Geographic
Image Collection
Page 660 F. Polking/Corbis/Contrasto
Page 661 J. Sweberg/Ardea
Page 662 D.A. Northcott/Corbis/
Contrasto
Page 663 F. Polking/Blickwinkel
Pages 664-665 S. Widstrand/Corbis/
Contrasto
Page 666 Y. Arthus-Bertrand/Corbis/
Contrasto
Page 667 D. Robert and L. Frantz/
Corbis/Contrasto
Page 668 K. Su/Alamy Images
Page 669 J. Zuckerman/Corbis/
Contrasto
Pages 670-671 J. Zuckerman/Corbis/
Contrasto
Page 672 Natural Visions
Page 673 T. Allofs/Corbis/Contrasto
Pages 674-675 T. Brakefield/Corbis/
Contrasto
Pages 676-677 J.M. Sanchez and
J.L. deLope
Pages 678-679 M. Quinton
Pages 680-681 R. Wittek/Blickwinkel
Pages 682-683 T. Davis/Corbis/
Contrasto
Pages 684-685 J. Syverson/Corbis/
Contrasto

Pages 686-687 D. Tardif/Corbis/
Contrasto
Pages 688-689 M. Harvey/Corbis/
Contrasto
Pages 690-691 E. Dragesco
Page 692 K. Su/China Span
Pages 692-693 Panda Photo
Pages 694-695 Panda Photo
Pages 696-697 S. Bloom Images/Alamy
Images
Pages 698-699 J. Rotman
Pages 700-701 J.P. Ferrero/Ardea
Pages 702-703 N. Rosing/National
Geographic Image Collection
Pages 704-705 Morales/Age
Fotostock/Contrasto
Page 706 S. Bloom Images/Alamy
Images
Page 707 T. Davis/Corbis/Contrasto
Page 708 Corbis/Contrasto
Page 709 M. Milanese
Pages 710-711 W. Dow/Corbis/
Contrasto
Page 712 F. Siteman/Age Fotostock/
Contrasto
Page 713 D. Magnin
Page 714 M. Milanese
Page 715 J. Daniels/Ardea
Pages 716-717 D. Husher
Pages 718-719 B. Lundberg/Nature
Picture Library
Pages 720-721 J. Eastcott/Y. Eastcott
Film/National Geographic Image
Collection
Pages 722-723 J. McDonald/Corbis/
Contrasto
Page 724 S. Danegger/NHPA
Page 725 J. Foxx/Alamy Images
Pages 726-727 Papilio/Alamy Images
Page 736 C. and M. Denis Huot

Africa. The tireless lion cubs consume most of their energy in playing.